Did You See the Moon Honey

Katie Dozier

&

Timothy Green

Did You See the Moon Honey: A Crown of Haibun
Copyright © 2025 by Katie Dozier & Timothy Green

Layout and editing by Timothy Green
Cover design by Timothy Green
Cover photo by Katie Dozier

ISBN: 978-1-961694-02-6

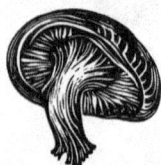

FUNGIBLE EDITIONS

First print edition by Fungible Editions
fungibleeditions.com

CONTENTS

Authors' Note

Much has happened since our last haibun crown—most notably, we're married! We closed the circle in February at Bok Tower Gardens in Florida, so this second crown covers not our honeymoon itself—which included trying to remember to sip a bit of honey mead every night—but our second moon as husband and wife.

Those golden days remain as sweet as our love for the haibun form, though, so the title fits, and the rules of the crown were the same as for last April's *Hot Pink Moon*: every day for National Poetry Month, we took turns writing a haibun using all of the words from the previous day's haiku. The last haiku in the series is built from the words in the text of the first haibun, bringing the crown of 30 full-circle. In that way, all of these poems are stitched together with a single unending thread.

We began the month apart, as we finished tying up loose ends across state lines, but finished teaching a workshop together at a rustic writers' retreat in Texas. The path in between was full of surprises as we danced between the earthly and the cosmic, curating meaning from the mysteries of life.

Tim was in a bit of a writing funk early on, but Katie doesn't believe in writer's block, so she sprang into the opening haibun like she springs into everything—headlong and full of energy. By the end, we were both reminded how much we love writing and doing everything together, including reminding each other to check out the night sky.

Tim & Katie

Did You See the Moon Honey

Emerald City

Each spring, somehow the same surprise:
how fast the charcoal outlines of trees
are crayoned over with every shade of green.
Wildflowers wave from the highway,
and baby ducks fuzz their way across the trail
to bob along the lake. Spring onions spice
the air, and the raindrops seem to float.
I'm convinced a caterpillar smiled at me
and a blue jay quoted Frost. But how
many daffodils did it take to plant
this yellow brick road?

> erasure poem
> I black out
> old windows

Renewing the Lease

The old windows in this house swing inward on their hinges like shutters, and metal blinds hang inside the outer frames, rattling at the slightest wind. All day they dance their slinky dance within the tiny box they're given. At night, they shimmy and shake and keep the ghosts awake. It's a constant movement, life. Sometimes I'd rather the calm of a blackout curtain, hung high from the ceiling, nothing coming in. Other times I let the poem begin.

    rental cabin
    only the moon
    not for sale

Looking into the Pond

Now, what was once Thoreau's cabin
is just bald dirt. Concrete pillars connected
by chains around packed earth. In the center,
the cold hearth stone. If there were any flowers,
I would mistake it for a grave. Long ago, he built
this two-year rental. He inked by candlelight.
Only the moon watched from a window,
until he wondered if it was not a window
but a mirror—his own white face
awash in light, glowing up there.
In the end, he published.
Put it all for sale.

>   behind
>   [every frame]
>   curation

A Sudden Loosening of Choice

The word *curation* shares its root with "to cure," and so a curator is a guardian of the sick from the wealth of the world. How we marvel as our words drag the clattering frames of their origins behind them. *Whiskey* is the water of life. *Mortgage* a death vow, the prance of a prank. In 1762, the 4th Earl of Sandwich needed a way to eat without leaving the gambling table. But now we prefer the thin blade of an omelet for lunch. What a tragedy we've found! What a goat song! But every disaster has its star. And who would smash a fiasco?

this feeling over abundance

Not Trying

Tonight, behind an iron arch
the hummingbird buzzes
as she considers building
her nest above our front door.
Her chirps are more like squeaks—
perhaps she fears the soon-to-open
beaks, or this biological electric storm
that forces her helicopter hovering
into as close to rest as she can muster.

     waning crescent
     no more new
     moons

At first, her eggs are an abundance of peas;
but the next day they outgrow her—
feeling how the murmur of life
is barely enough to slow her.

Sea Urchins

Note how the two moons on this new planet appear in perfect opposition. That, too, is a kind of harmony. As the waxing moon rises, the waning moon sets. As the gibbous cup of one disc grows full, the other one empties from the crescent that it lacks. They lie at the far ends of each horizon, shouting inverted stories. But add them together: there is no more darkness than there is light. That's a metaphor we've saved for the poets. They should be arriving on the next ship.

> low tide
> the pull of your weight
> in the distance

Margin Trading

My brain likes to swirl around the most when it should
stay still. Here it happens again, while taking off my clothes
at the dermatologist. I am wondering how many empty
Tides have been swept up in the tide, as though plastic
can have a sense of humor. I don't know why I think
of half the things I do but it doesn't make me any less
sure of them. They take my weight, pull my hair to
scrape around my scalp. A fluorescent light flickers
as though snapping at me, and what is the opposite
of snapping? Your arms around me; how they never
let go first. Out the window, pine needles blow
around down low—how it is to feel
my distance from the earth.

finding people's good sides Mohs surgery

Too Soft

My eyes didn't widen in finding that the last rock in the Mohs hardness kit they handed out in 8th grade Earth Science was a real diamond. I didn't imagine the simple surgery of extracting its riches from the bottom cubby of the wooden bento box it came in, or how it would feel, heavy and hard in my side pocket. I couldn't conceive of selling it in an alley behind the 7-Eleven and buying all the things I always wanted but never had. I was one of the good people. So when the teacher explained that it was industrial grade and practically worthless, I wasn't even relieved.

> gypsum, calcite, quartz …
> we impress no one
> above ourselves

Rarity

At the natural history museum, the hall of minerals
is full of lit up rocks—showgirls twirling, each inside
a different black box. The pink quartz would curtsey
if she could unpeg herself; the green calcite crystal
ladies swirl, tipsy in their column dresses, and
gypsum is spotlit in her see-through slip. Above
their cases, descriptions that impress:
"one of the largest specimens," by
a roped-off wall of amethyst, but no
confessions by those shards that are
second best. We wander room to
room, anthropomorphizing all—
hoping to crack the geode
of ourselves.

> mining
> the universe
> for you

The Space of a Second

From the office window, I catch a four-step glimpse of you crossing the yard, a trowel and hand fork hanging at your hip, a bag of seeds tucked under one arm, two girls trailing behind, and I think of gardening as the opposite of mining. How it's tending rather than taking. Not pulling from the earth, but pushing off against it. Helping beauty reach for the edge of the universe. For a moment it all makes sense.

feeling the pulsar on my wrist

Leaving the Light On

I had to look up *pulsar,* and found a star
pulsing beams of electromagnetic radiation—
which must look like when you followed me
home and I held my hand out the car window,
feeling the sun's heat so with a wave of my wrist
you could watch the diamonds you gave me glitter
on my ring finger from a car-length away. Much
the same, a pulsar's gamma rays can only be seen
if they are pointing your way; which answers the
"if a tree falls in the forest" cliché.

>reading
>a poem out loud
>jump start!

The Anthropic Principle

The first time I jump-started a car, dead as a brick in a Denny's parking lot, I didn't know how much it mattered not to get the wires reversed. I remembered reading the manual—that red was positive, and black was the cable to ground—but the terminals on the old Chevy were so corroded that their labels had vanished. Dusting the lid with a sleeve, I peered into the salty flakes and sea-green goo like an archeologist trying to pull an ancient poem from crumbling papyrus, shrugged, and clipped the ends on wherever. I can't even call it a guess. If I had thought first, I'd have figured the layout matched my friend's Buick, that right was negative, which must have been wrong. Instead, I called out for him to fire it up, whooped loud, and drove off into another year of ignorance.

spring
-ing off the bike path!
squirrels

Requiem

Spring has been springing so much.
Even the blue is green. The coursing
wind's a heartbeat; branches arc out
and back in, above our bike path.
Flying squirrels are a hoot, spot one
as it glides behind another magnolia.
Even the cardinals chirp in high-C.
Nature presents as only she can:
ringed by her own impermanence—
one toppling bud Jengas the whole
composition. But from the ground,
with no more spinning wheels to
cycle through these remaining years—
all of this must be permanent.

      every note
      a memento
      mori

A Period

at the end of a sentence is what makes the meaning, he said,
mean though it is, and hard as a peppercorn rattling at the
bottom of a glass vial through which the words *memento mori*
form a hidden skull in the corner of the note on the empty table
where an otherwise blank sheet of waxy vellum is illuminated
only by a single candle tunneled into the glossy pool of its own
melting in the same way that a great star collapses into the
bottomless weight of its impossible mass, a black eye unblinking
around which everything swirls, you and me, the bulbs in bloom
and the ones that won't all falling forever but never finally
reaching that one dark dot at the edge of the wind exhaled in the
sentence, without which

> fever dream
> all the dawns
> in palimpsest

After Poems

The paper used to be more valuable than the text—
the solution? Palimpsest. Just scrape the words off

and watch the letters swirl into the dust of a dream—
color the sky lavender at twilight. I know what it is

to be erased. So much of beauty is in the threat
of being lost. These days, I find it hard to walk away

from sandcastles. Fevers, unrecorded, could be confused
with warmth. Speeds, left unrecorded, could rocket faster

than the sun. Invisible to pink erasers, nearly all my words
will live on in the cloud of this machine—

seeds dying to sprout, mostly unseen.

    ghost craters
        [   ]
    forgotten inspiration

Narrative Spirit

The summer after the divorce, my brother and I shared a room in my grandmother's house, a Sears kit home her father built with his own hands in the 1920s. My aunt told me the house was haunted by his ghost, and that was all the inspiration I needed. I saw him myself that first night, standing at the end of my bed, a terrible glowing specter that hovered, then hovered away down the hall. Of course it was only Grandma in her white robe, checking in on us half-asleep. But by morning, she'd forgotten getting up. *Don't mind the past,* she said, heaping another pile of hash browns onto our breakfast plates. *It's all just craters on the moon.*

> a slight glimmer
> added to the scales
> fish story

The Deep-Sea Angler

At the poker table, some are proud to be fish.
They school about—silver-backed cards, desperate
to outwit the sharks. They dart around the bluffs,
one eye squinting through the muck. Better to
be an octopus. Have enough hands to pattycake
those fish, give them a slight glimmer of their wish.
Sharks gobble—forget to leave a single scale. But
before I take, my suckers have added to their story—
offering a tale of a mermaid for bait. But in the end,
all of us are just pulled in the pot. The ocean's rake.

> winning
> the tournament
> bioluminescence

Deep Scattering

Consider the lanternfish. About the size of a paperclip, but a half-trillion tons of them spilled in a layer of the twilight zone. When the naval soundmen send their blooping pings into the ocean's depths, they bleep back off the gassy bladders of these tiny fish in a phantom bed that rises in the night and falls every morning. At the same time, on their slender bellies, in beads of bioluminescence, a blue glow mimics the surface of the sea. False floor and false ceiling, they've been fooling us all since the Eocene. And yet we think we're winning the tournament.

echo sounding
in the train tunnel
footfalls

Pounding

Sounding: I heard you for years before
I knew you. Running down the escalator
to catch the last train out; chef's whites
and my aching feet in black clogs—
leather footfalls on the moving metal.
Halfway down your voice said *stop*
and I grabbed the arm rail, still a hundred
feet up, just fast enough to keep me from
tumbling when the escalator became
stairs. *Stop* echoed in the night air.
But the station was empty. No faces;
no crowd. Just that familiar apparition
of sound. I rained onto the platform,
the tunnel's white ceiling grooved
like clusters of upside-down tables—
a clattering of cutlery making a bell
out of my head. What was it the new
dishwasher had said? Wet hands all
day make our hands so dry at night.
The train screeches in. Still alive.

    knowing
    for the first time
    mortar & pestle

Apothecary

For the first time, we climb out together and sit on the granite ledge. Three holes here the size of soup bowls. They're either evidence of an ancient riverbed, where a floodwater's eddies turned tumbling rocks into tiny drill bits. Or they're grinding stones the Serrano peoples used as mortar and pestle to crush acorns into flour. Once the meal was milled, they'd let it soak in the sun to leach away the bitter tannins. Without knowing, my daughter empties her pockets of the leaves and flowers she's collected and mashes them with a rock. She offers up the powder like a medicine, and I take it.

    at the back of the drawer
    another memory
    to dust

Taps

We can't pick what we write about.
You can't drown water. You can't
lock it in a drawer. Whether a soak,
or well-sugared tea, evaporation is full
of emptiness. Memories are rubber
ducks that spring up. Bubbles pop
because they cling too hard to
something. My back hurts again.
It may as well be a fiberglass hull.
The light slices through the blinds;
the dust swirls back—a kind of map.
Another chance to bemoan this fact:
the dirt is coming for me. But in the
meantime, I'll clean the chandelier.

> bath bomb …
> all that glitters
> makes a mess

Pittsburgh

After bombing at my first and only folk concert, I took what still might be my final bubble bath. I wasn't crestfallen, climbing into the oversized tub, just cold. I had to hoof it all the way up Squirrel Hill from the warehouse district where I'd played, my guitar case clenched in one frozen claw, a useless second-hand amp under the other arm. Fat flakes of late snow, the kind that glitters, were a confetti all around me. The bubbles came with the room. A small bottle on a wicker tray next to a sliver of soap. I poured it in as the water rose and disappeared beneath the mess a dare makes. The steam swirled. I never understood why I was happy in that moment, having failed so fully. Meanwhile, outside the fogging window, somewhere far downstream, you must have been seventeen.

> three rivers
> finally meeting
> the one

Neurodivergent

Sometimes in the shower, I catch
myself singing *Pocahontas*, "you
can't step in the same river twice."
Well what's so unique about rivers?
Will she finally see us if we jump in
three more times? Now I understand
the beauty of bird watching—for me,
it's not enough to say a cardinal's red
when a Ferrari speeds by. While meeting
therapists, her tantrums paint fire-engines
on the floor. But nail polish bottles
are the best at names. "I Just Can't
Cope Acabana" shouts from my fingers.
Sakura's so pink that my eyes dissolve her
cotton candy, and green helps me
swing on the one
strong vine.

> asking her
> favorite color
> sea turtle

No Dumping

Three turtles on a log are a line of bongo drums. Red-eared sliders, her favorite, that color of sunset down their necks. Like the sky, they play themselves without asking. Plop, plop, plop. No one tells them all this drains to the sea.

lingering rain on the roof of your mouth

Checking the Farmers' Almanac

Some roofs make me wish for a storm—
perhaps this is the humor of modern life;
the urge to hear the rain rattle on the roof,
but from inside, not wet, but warm—
another mouth. Don't we just make a new
womb from every room: this one has floral
wallpaper, climbing to the ceiling. Lingering
vines always have a reason. Wildflowers in the
median could be random, could be seeds
sprayed out of the side of a truck last
season. But either way, for us, look
at all the irises. It has
rained luck.

> honeymoon …
> the sun
> never sets

Perennials

It's not a honeymoon, they say, but moon honey, drizzled thick from a dipper turned on the sun's lathe. May a large drop fall on your days and cover you with a sweetness that sticks to everything—the thin handle of the steel spoon, the counter where your mind sets it, the cup, your thumbprint stuck to its lip in a sugary glaze. May the plastic pump of the soap dispenser, the knob on the cabinet door where the towels hang, stay rough with that touch and never be clean. That's how the moon hangs. It turns and it returns. It slides into shadow, and the shadow fades. But did you see the moon, honey? How it wears its wounds in the open while it glows.

> rain lilies
> in a wild field
> curing

Buried

Curing wild salmon
requires a sharp knife,
and the will to poke
the blade in behind
the skin. Just right.
This cutting in—
the chance to make
the most of what is last.
I rain the salt down
atop the salmon's side,
with sugar and fresh dill,
while from the field
outside, the lilies
crane their crowns
to peek inside—
the flowers of
rebirth.

> geocache
> hunting
> for you

Lightning Ridge

I wonder how many times I've come across a geocache while out hiking and didn't know it. Strange things on the trails in the back canyons. Painted rocks, stacks of coins, a small plane, the wreck of a car's twisted frame. Hunting for nothing but fresh air, I found a bracelet once, in a wooden box under a fallen log the wind had worn smooth. Gold and vine-like, *for you, always*, it said in a flowery script. But I knew it wasn't for me. Not yet. So I left it there in the dirt, overlooking the yucca and the pines.

rediscovering paradise lost and found

Genesis

I never thought of paradise
as palm trees, as glowing sand,
as falling asleep on a pink towel—
with an umbrella'd coconut
somehow in my hand. No,
a place like paradise just
couldn't stand to sit still.
And that must be why
we're two hummingbirds
flitting from the beach
to a rainbow field of zinnias—
and here we hover
for our little wingspan
of time; rediscovering
nectar when we thought
all the sweetness had
scattered. Lost. But
look around at how
we keep finding
flowers. Now
buzzing as
we forget
the frost.

       eating
       the forbidden fruit
       poet tree

Your True Nature

There's nothing forbidden to a poet—not on the page. Plant the word *tree* and already its feeder roots are drinking in the cracks of a melting tundra. They chisel away at the drip line, and above them, the heavy boughs gnarl to the far edge of the margin. A tree like that, its limbs outstretched, is asking to be climbed, and you do, shimmying over rough bark toward the heart, higher and higher up its impossible trunk, until it isn't an oak anymore but an entire orchard, intertwined, bearing in bounty all the fruits that you've touched but never tasted. No one needs to describe them. Curved as they are, shaped in their shape, and soft in that delicate hue. No one says that you're eating them. Then you do.

> every shade
> convinced me
> caterpillar

About the Authors

Timothy Green is the editor of *Rattle* magazine, a fact which Katie Dozier is grateful for—particularly as he published her first poem in print before they ever met! Timothy grew up in Rochester, New York, and became known as the dude whose car doubled as a used sporting goods store. Katie bounced around the South in her early years, and kicked off a poker career while studying poetry at Florida State University. Years later, thanks to Tim's tireless promotion of unpretentious poetry with the weekly *Rattlecast* and *Critique of the Week*—and Katie's desire to be the best poet possible—they found each other! Now, Katie is associate editor for her favorite poetry magazine, and co-hosts the Prompt Lines on the *Rattlecast*. She also hosts and produces the *The Poetry Space_*, which Tim co-hosts. They enjoy speaking at conferences, leading workshops, and going for long bike rides on the trails in The Woodlands, Texas. This is the second book of the 1,000 they will write together.

www.ingramcontent.com/pod-product-compliance
Lightning Source LLC
LaVergne TN
LVHW051431080426
835508LV00022B/3341